The Nutritive Relations Of The Surrounding Tissues To The Archegonia In Gymnosperms

Marie Carmichael Stopes

In the interest of creating a more extensive selection of rare historical book reprints, we have chosen to reproduce this title even though it may possibly have occasional imperfections such as missing and blurred pages, missing text, poor pictures, markings, dark backgrounds and other reproduction issues beyond our control. Because this work is culturally important, we have made it available as a part of our commitment to protecting, preserving and promoting the world's literature. Thank you for your understanding.

With the compliments of the authors.

The Nutritive Relations
of the surrounding Tissues to the Archegonia
in Gymnosperms.

By

M. C. Stopes

and

K. Fujii.

Reprinted from the Beihefte zum Botanischen Centralblatt
Bd. XX Heft 1.

Dresden
1906.

The nutritive relations of the surrounding tissues to the Archegonia in Gymnosperms.

By

M. C. Stopes, D. Sc., Ph. D.
Assistant Lecturer in Botany, University of Manchester,

and

K. Fujii, Ph. D.
Assistant Professor of Botany, Imperial University of Tokyo.

With plate I.

As regards the physiology of nutrition in the egg cells of Gymnosperms but little is to be found in the literature, but the socalled „protein vacuoles" and protein granules lying in the cytoplasm of the egg, have attracted the attention of various authors.

Hofmeister[1]) first called attention to the protein vacuoles under the name „Keimbläschen". He took them for cells formed by free cell formation and thought that from one of them the embryo arose. Schacht[2]) however recognised them as vacuoles and speaks of them in his text as „Scheinzellen (vacuolen)" and says (p. 399) that these structures „die ich nicht für wahre Zellen, sondern für Vacuolen oder Scheinzellen halte", have not the nature Hofmeister assigned to them. Strasburger[3]) also thought that they had the nature of vacuoles, and as they contained protein grains he spoke of them under the name „Eiweiss-Vacuolen". Goroschankin[4]) on the other hand says of these bodies that they „keine Vacuolen sind (wie Strasburger (sic) meint), sondern grosse Ähnlichkeit mit Zellkernen besitzen".[5])

---

[1]) Hofmeister, W., „Vergleich. Unters. d. Keimung etc. höherer Kryptog. ... u. d. Samenbildung d. Coniferen". Leipzig 1851. p. 130—131 and 140.

[2]) Schacht, H., „Lehrbuch d. Anat. u. Physiol. d. Gewächse". Zweiter Teil. Berlin 1859. p. 398—400.

[3]) Strasburger, E., „Neue Untersuch. ü. d. Befruchtungsorg. b. d. Phanerog.". 1884. p. 50.

[4]) Goroschankin, J., „Ueb. d. Korpuskeln u. d. Geschlechtsprocess d. Gymnospermen". 1880.

[5]) Goroschankin, J., Ueb. d. Befrucht.-Prozess bei *Pinus Pumilio*. Strassburg 1883. p. 3.

Hirase[1]) having seen similar protein granules in the jacket cells and in the egg cells of *Ginkgo* thought that the protein in the egg came as such from the jacket cells, though he figured wide pits in the egg cell wall, each closed by a simple membrane. In *Cycas* Ikeno[2]) thought that the nuclei of the jacket cells become homogeneous and break off part of their substance which enters the egg cell. As he did not observe the "sieve" perforations in the egg cell wall described by Goroschankin he holds the view that there is a wide, open communication between the egg cell and the sheath cells through which he figures this protein substance passing.

Blackman[3]) and, at one time Chamberlain[4]), followed Strasburger's view and considered the „Hofmeister Körperchen" to be merely protein vacuoles.

Arnoldi[5]) investigated the origin of these bodies in the Abietineae, concluding that they are the nuclei of the jacket cells which have passed bodily into the egg. According to him these nuclei are replaced in the jacket cells by others coming in from the surrounding endosperm cells. In *Cephalotaxus* and *Dammara* he describes protein originating in the nuclei of the sheath cells and passing into the egg. He brings together a series of Gymnosperms and states that in all cases the protein vacuoles and granules in the egg arise directly or indirectly from the nuclei of the jacket cells. Arnoldi's results however have not been confirmed by Murril[6]) in *Tsuga*, Ferguson[7]) in *Pinus*, Miyake[8]) in *Picea* and *Abies*, Land[9]) in *Thuja*, or Sludsky[10]) in *Juniperus*, and were even denied by Strasburger[11]).

---

[1]) Hirase, S., „Etudes s. l. fécondation et l'embryolog. d. *Ginkgo biloba*. (Journ. of the Coll. of Sci. Imp. Univ.". Tokio. Vol. VIII. 1895. Plate XXXI, fig. 6 and p. 12.)

[2]) Ikeno, S., „Untersuch. ü. d. Entwick. ... b. *Cycas revoluta*". (Jahrb. f. wiss. Bot. XXXII. 1898. p. 557—600. Plate 8 fig. 7b.)

[3]) Blackman, V. H., „The cytolog. features of fertiliz. and related phenom. in *Pinus sylvestris*". (Phil. Trans. Roy. Soc. Lond. Ser. B. 190. 1898. p. 395—642. see p. 417.)

[4]) Chamberlain, C. J., „Oogenesis in *Pinus Laricio*". (Bot. Gaz. 27. 1899. p. 268 to 280. see p. 273.)

[5]) Arnoldi, W., „Beit. z. Morph. d. Gymnosp.". IV. (Flora. Bd. 87. 1900. see p. 4.)

[6]) Murril, W. A., „The develop. of the Archeg. and fertiliz. in the Hemlockspruce *(Tsuga canadensis)*. (Ann. of Botany. 14. 1900. p. 5—83.)

[7]) Ferguson, M. C., „Contrib. to the know. of the life hist. of *Pinus*". (Proc. of the Washington Acad. of Sci. Sept. 1904. Vol. VI. p. 1—202. see p. 104.)

[8]) Miyake, K., „On the develop. of the sexual organs and fertiliz. in *Picea excelsa*". (Ann. of Bot. 17. 1903. p. 351.) „Contrib. to fertiliz. and embryog. of *Abies balsamea*". (Beiheft. z. Bot. Centralbl. 14. 1903. p. 134.)

[9]) Land, W. J. G., „A morph. study of Thuja". (Bot. Gaz. 1902. p. 249—258.)

[10]) Sludsky, N., „Ueber d. Entwicklungsgeschichte d. *Juniperus communis*". (B. d. D. Bot. Ges. Bd. 23. 1905. Heft 5. p. 214.)

[11]) Strasburger, E., „Ueber Plasmaverbindungen pflanzlicher Zellen". (Jahrb. f. wiss. Bot. Vol. 36. 1901. p. 550—552.)

Coker[1]) in his work on *Taxodium* described fragmentation of the jacket cell nuclei and favoured Ikeno's and Arnoldi's views that the protein vacuoles appearing in the egg cell originate from their substance which passes in through the pitted egg cell wall. Coulter and Chamberlain[2]) in their recent book assume the proteid vacuoles to be nuclei.

Smith[3]) in *Zamia floridana* called the main pit filling cytoplasm on the side of the egg which is very granular „haustoria" to which she ascribed pumping action and periods of accumulation, discharge, and exhaustion in the process of absorbing food. Stating however at the same time „No sieve plates or similar structures as described by Goroschankin were observed in any of the preparations", she drew all her figures with the pits between the egg and jacket cells as simple broad open communications.

Stopes[4]) figured simple closed pits in *Zamia muricata*; and in the course of work on many species of Cycads found no case of the fragmentation or wandering of the nuclei of the jacket cells, but supported Hirase's results for *Ginkgo* rather than Ikeno's for *Cycas* in regard to the protein granules in the egg.

Ferguson[5]) in her monograph on *Pinus* used the term "nutritive spheres" in place of "proteid vacuoles" and suggested the theory that the nucleoli of the jacket cells and egg cells have somewhat the nature of plastids and manufacture "secondary nucleoli" which "become diffused throughout the nucleus, from which they pass, probably in solution, into the egg cytoplasm. Here they are again differentiated, and by a gradual development give rise to the „proteid vacuoles" or nutritive spheres of the oosphere". In Mottier's[6]) summary of the whole subject, he states the views of various authors, and questions the fact that „the material should pass over bodily into the egg cell" as being „an extraordinary mode of passage of foodstuffs".

Treub's[7]) original figures of the thickened membrane of the Cycad archegonia shewing a closing membrane across simple pits between the egg and the jacket cells, and Goroschankin's sieve-like communications are in general overlooked by recent workers, with the result that many consider that protein in solid or semi-solid form, or even complete nuclei, may enter the egg cell. On the other hand, Ferguson failed to observe even the larger pits in *Pinus* and so favours the view that in this case only soluble

---

[1]) Coker, W. C., „On the gametophytes and embryo of *Taxodium*". (Bot. Gaz. Vol. 36. 1903. p. 25.)
[2]) Coulter, J. M., and Chamberlain, C. J., „Morph. of Spermatophytes. Part I. Gymnosperms". New York 1901. p. 22 and 88.
[3]) Smith, I. S., „Nutrition of the egg in *Zamia*". (Bot. Gaz. Vol. 37. 1904. p. 347.)
[4]) Stopes, M. C., „Beitr. z. Kennt. d. Fortpflanz. d. Cycadeen". (Flora. Bd. 93 1904. p. 479. fig. 16.)
[5]) Ferguson, M. C., loc. cit. p. 104 and 107.
[6]) Mottier, D. M., „Fecundation in plants". Washington 1904. see p. 44.
[7]) Treub, M., „Recherches s. l. Cycadées". (Ann. d. Jard. d. Buitenzorg. Vol. IV. see figs. 7 and 8 pl. II.)

food enters. Our work has impressed on us the remarkable uniformity in the structure of the thickened wall in all the Cycads, *Ginkgo*, and *Pinus* in which the big pits are closed by a final lamella which can normally only allow soluble or semi-soluble food to pass.

All recent workers appear to unite in turning finally to the nuclei of the jacket cells as the factory of protein nourishment for the egg cell, and do not carry the question further. Thus ignoring the possible activities of the jacket cells themselves and their work as agents between the original supply of various food substances and the growing egg in which the food is required in a form available for immediate utilization.

Materials and their treatment.

In the course of our investigations up to the present we have examined the following species: *Cycas Beddomei, C. circinalis, C. Normanbyana, C. revoluta,* and *C.* sp.?, *Zamia floridana, Z. integrifolia, Z. muricata* and *Z.* sp.?, *Ceratozamia fusco-viridis, C. mexicana, C. Miqueliana, Macrozamia Preissii, M. spiralis, Encephalartos Hildebrandtii, E. horridus, E. Lehmanni* and *E.* sp.?, *Dioon edule, Stangeria schizodon, Ginkgo biloba, Pinus Cembra, P. montana, P. Pinea* and *P. sylvestris*.

In this first part of our work we have used for fixing Flemmings strong solution diluted with an equal volume of water; Alcohol acetic; Chrom-acetic; and various strengths of Alcohol alone. In the case of the Cycads the best preservation of the structure of the egg cytoplasm without shrinkage was observed after using 90 % alcohol, fixing the whole seed even when the stone layers had considerably hardened. For digestion experiments with pepsin also 90 % alcohol proved to be the best fixative. With Flemming's fixative we found that a very strong reducing substance present in the tissues caused excessive deposit of reduced osmium, and the results were not always satisfactory. With *Pinus*, particularly *P. Cembra*, where the endosperm is very large, we got excellent preservation of the structure of the egg cytoplasm by separating the endosperm from the integuments and nucellus, fixing in 30 % Alcohol and then slowly transferring to higher percentages of alcohol.

We also always examined fresh material whenever it was possible, for many of the substances which are important in the process of nutrition such as oxydases, sugars etc., cannot be dealt with in fixed material.

For paraffin embedding we used Cedar oil chiefly (sometimes chloroform) between the Absolute Alcohol and paraffin. Microtome series were stained with Flemmings triple stain, acetic methyl green (with or without the addition of Sodium sulphate) Congo red, ruthenium red, and other stains, or treated with aqueous solution of iodine, alcoholic solution of iodine in potassium iodide, Millon's reagent, or Chlorzinc Iodine as the case demanded. Microtome series treated with Iodine yielded particularly instructive results when compared with similar series stained with Triple stain, especially as regards the starch and protein grains. For the detection of "plasmodesmen" we chiefly used hand sections of 90 % spirit material.

In short we used as many kinds of material as were available, checking the results obtained from hand sections of fresh material with those of microtome series whenever possible.

Observations.

Cycads.

The general appearance of the Cycadean prothallium, with its large archegonia, is too well known to require special description. The cells of the prothallium immediately surrounding the egg cell differ somewhat in appearcance from the others and have long been known under the name of "jacket" or „sheath" cells. In all the Cycads we have examined these cells appear to be simply modified cells of the prothallium, and no facts have come to light in our work to support Lawson's[1]) view (expressed for *Sequoia* and *Cryptomeria*) that they are reduced sterile eggs. This however does not affect their physiological relation to the egg cell which is our present consideration.

The facts that the ir cytoplasm is very thick and granular, and their nuclei are frequently twice or more in diameter those of ordinary endosperm cells (see fig. 8) already indicated the pysiological importance of the jacket cells, which we must discuss later after various details have been brought forward.

In the course of this paper we will attempt to describe the observations made on the nature of food stuffs entering the Archegonia (not only the protein granules to which most authors confine their attention, but also carbohydrates etc.), the form in which these food stuffs travel, and the mode of their passage through the cell walls.

The youngest fresh material of Cycads which we have examined was *Ceratozamia fusco-viridis*, in which the egg cells were only just recognisable with the naked eye. By this time starch was laid down in the integuments, and to a slight extent in the nucellus, but the thin walled, hyaline endosperm tissues were entirely devoid of it. On testing whole endosperms with Fehling's solution, strong reduction took place as was seen by the considerable formation of cuprous oxide; this reaction, although suggesting the presence of sugar is not necessarily conclusive, as there is a strong "reducing substance[2]) other than known kinds of sugars, present in large

---

[1]) Lawson, A. A., „The gametophytes, archegonia, fertilization and embryo of *Sequoia sempervirens*". (Ann. of Bot. Vol. XVIII. 1904. p. 1 to 28. see p. 15.) „The gamet., fertiliz. and emb. of *Cryptomeria Japonica*". (Ann. of Bot. Vol. XVIII. 1904. p. 417 to 444. see p. 431.)

[2]) Fujii, K., „Ueber d. Bestäubungstropfen d. Gymnospermen". (Berichte d. D. Bot. Ges. Bd. XXI. 1903. Heft 4. p. 215.)

quantities in the endosperm. That the cells of the endosperm were rich in sugar was established by heating drops of sap obtained from them by means of capillary tubes, with an aqueous solution of acetate of phenylhydrazin after the method of one of us[1]), or by heating sections of the tissues with the same reagent in small open tubes. On cooling, the characteristic crystals of gluc-ozozone developed in large quantities, proving that there must have been much glucose in the tissues. Cane sugar did not seem to be present to any recognisable extent. To test this, sections were placed in a strong aqueous solution of Invertin for $1^1/_2$ hours and then tested with acetate of phenylhydrazin, but there was no noticeable increase in the quantity of ozozone crystals formed; while in the control experiments carried on at the same time with a weak solution of cane sugar with the addition of invertin even after 10 minutes we got very well marked formation of glucozozone crystals.

Oxydases were present in the vascular bundles of the Integuments, apparently in the phloem, perhaps coinciding with the "Leptomin" had been found by Raciborski[2]) in this position in many plants. In the jacket cells it appeared also to be pesent, but was difficult to demonstrate exactly owing to the presence of the already mentioned reducing substance in the surrounding endosperm cells which we found hindered the reaction of guajac resin.

In other materials of an allied species of *Ceratozamia* just a little older than the above, the same facts held good, except that the carbohydrates were not only present in a soluble form (sugars) but also had begun to be deposited in the form of small starch grains in the endosperm cells towards the base of the Archegonia.

Protein substance also appeared to be supplied in a soluble form at this stage, the nucellus showed very strong protein reactions with Millon's reagent, Iodine (which was applied in alcoholic solution to sections previously treated with absolute alcohol to prevent the reaction of starch) and biuret reaction. In the general endosperm cells the reaction was faint though definite, while in the jacket cells and their nuclei the reactions were more apparent. In this stage we could not observe any definite granules such as were readily detectable in the later stages when protein storage begins in the endosperm. In many Cycads the deposition of protein substance in solid form appears to lag behind that of the starch in and near the egg, but this seems to be reversed in the case of *Ginkgo* where the well developed protein grains appear very early in the egg cell.

---

[1]) Fujii, K., „Kleinere Beiträge z. Mikrotechnik". „An. d. Glaskapillar z. mikrochem. Analyse". (Compte Rendu d. séan. d. 6 Congres intern. d. Zool. (Berne 1904). Genève 1905. p. 531.)

[2]) Raciborski, M., „Ein Inhaltskörper d. Leptoms". (Berichte d. D. Bot. Ges. Bd. XVI. 1898. p. 52—63.) „Weitere Mitteil. ü. d. Leptomin". (loc. cit. p. 119 and 123.) „Einige Demonstrationsversuche mit Leptomin". (Flora. Bd. 85. 1898. p. 362 to 367.)

If we follow the history of the starch deposition in an older series of ovules, for example in a series of *Zamia floridana*. We find the following course of events. The first deposition of starch takes place in the cells of the endosperm just at the base of the Archegonia, this spreads up the sides of the Archegonia leaving the jacket cells empty, but soon appearing in the neck cells where some grains are almost always found up till the time of fertilization. In the course of the following month the amount of starch deposited in the endosperm cells steadily increases in quantity and in the size of the grains. In the jacket, the cells at the base of the archegonium are the first to be filled with starch grains and gradually nearly all the cells of the jacket layer become packed. A little later this starch is again dissolved away while yet the egg cell and endosperm cells are well filled with grains (cf. fig. 5),[1]. In the egg cell the starch appeared at first almost entirely at the perifery, and this before they are deposited in the jacket layer. These grains vary somewhat in size but are very much smaller than those in the endosperm cells, only in one exceptional case were they equally large.

In egg cells about 2.6 to 3 mm long, the small starch grains frequently appeared to be associated with protein grains which in this stage were not deposited in the cells just near the egg cell but were present in large quantities in those somewhat removed from it. In further developed eggs about this size the appearance of the starch and protein grains was very striking. In the egg cell itself were present both starch and protein, the starch in very minute grains, the protein substance being deposited in rather irregular, sometimes considerably complicated masses of very various sizes. There were very few or no protein granules in the jacket cells, and little in those cells of the endosperm adjoining the jacket layer. In the rest of the endosperm, the cells contained large quantities of protein, many of the grains being large and irregular exactly like those of the egg cell. In the cells further removed from the egg cell the granules tended to become finer and finer, till the region was reached in which the protein appeared to have filled the bulk of the cell in a viscous or semifluid condition which in the fixed material shewed spaces of bubble like appearance. Thus the deposition of protein grains began first in the cells near the egg, and in the egg itself as is also always the case with starch. In later stages the cells nearer the egg cell appeared empty of protein grains (cf. figs 7 and 8 of the same thing in *Ginkgo*) which had been re-dissolved for the use of the growing egg.

A similar arrangement was seen in the case of the starch. In the egg cell itself there were large numbers of extremely fine roundish

---

[1]) It is interesting to note that such as stage had been figured by Warming in *Ceratozamia robusta*, though he did not attach any importance to it. Résumé. „Rech. et. rem. s. l. Cycadées". Tab. II. fig. 15. (Overs. d. Kon. Danske Vid. Selsk. 1877.)

grains scattered throughout the whole cytoplasm as well as in a definite zone just at the perifery where they were so thickly clustered as to make an almost solid black band round the edge of the egg when stained with Iodine. When examined with an oil immersion lens these small round grains appeared in general clustered together in groups from 2 to 10 or 20; each group appearing to be formed in one leucoplast (cf. fig. 6) but there were also a few single larger grains lying in the cytoplasm separate from the others. The starch grains in the egg were different in character and appearance from those in the endosperm cells. In general they stained rather brownish violet which shews that they contained amylodextrine. Some of the grains in the endosperm cells next to the empty jacket layer were also more brownish staining and smaller, probably in a partly dissolved condition, while the rest of the endosperm was packed with large, brightly bluish-violet staining grains of storage starch which later on were also dissolved to supply the egg. Thus the zone of emptying cells travels continually outwards from the egg cells, leaving a zone of empty cells immediately round them. We do not find that these empty cells are disintegrating or abnormal in any way, they are merely deprived of their own stores and then serve as the path of transmission for the food stuffs from the other cells to the egg cell. They and their nuclei retain their integrity throughout this stage of passage of food to the egg.

Similar facts have been observed in various other species of Cycads. In *Macrozamia spiralis* however the deposition of the protein grains appears to preceed that of the starch, for in young egg cells we found many large protein grains scattered thickly through the whole substance of the egg cell, while the starch was only just beginning to be deposited in a few of the endosperm cells at the base of the Archegonia. In the jacket cells we observed also small protein grains which had the appearance of so called "extra nucleolar nucleoli" when stained with triple stain and to which we will refer again. For this species of *Macrozamia* we had only alcohol material, but so far as we could judge the sugar present appeared to be cane sugar, at least in the stage we examined, for we got many gluc-ozozone crystals formed by the acetate of phenylhydrazin test only when the test was made after the inversion process had been previously carried on. In this species the starch grains appear in the perifery of the egg rather later than usual.

In later stages of all the species of Cycads examined, the starch again disappears from the egg cell as well as from the sheath cells and the immediately surrounding endosperm cells, as it is turned into soluble carbohydrates and used by the growing egg.

In the ripening seed, the quantity of starch in the endosperm, as is well known, is very great except in the zone just by the egg cell. The cells however cannot be described as "full of starch" as there is such a large quantity of protein substance in definite grains that when tested with Millon's reagent the endosperm becomes the deepest crimson. This is particularly noticeable in *Dioon* and *Encephalartos*, but holds good for all species examined.

The formation of starch grains in the egg cell from the plentiful supply of sugar is readily explained by the presence of plastids which we observed there in large numbers, but the formation of solid protein grains in the egg is not so simply explained. We endeavoured to obtain some information as to the nature of these protein grains in different parts of the tissues by the use of artificial pepsin digestion.[1]) For this we found *Macrozamia spiralis*, in which the protein grains in the egg are large, and those in the jacket cells similar to them, very good material. We used hand sections of alcohol material well washed in water and treated with a mixture of 3 parts · 3% H.Cl in H_2O + 1 part pepsin glycerine, and kept in this digestive fluid at a temperature of about $40\,^\circ$ C. After treatment for 14 hours the protein granules in the egg, and nearly all those in the jacket cells had lost their high refraction and become "ghostly" remnants of their former selves with little or none of their previous active staining power. The chromatin bodies of the egg nucleus however became much more brilliantly refractive than before (as is characteristic of chromatin after such treatment) while the nucleolus of the egg cell became slightly granular in appearance. In other cases, after 21 hours the protein granules of the egg cell and most of those in the jacket cells were completely digested, the nucleoli of the egg and jacket cells remaining undigested, with a few other small grains.

This result proves that the nucleoli and protein grains are different in chemical structure so that one can hardly look to the nucleoli of the jacket layer as their direct source as some authors have done. So also the fact that protein grains just like those of the egg exist in extremely large quantities in the endosperm cells makes it difficult to think that the nucleoli alone should build them up. It seems to us rather that the protein substance accumulates in the endosperm cells, entering in soluble and probably simpler forms, and that in both egg and endosperm cells it is rebuilt in a semiviscous state, when it begins to concentrate, forming granules. The large irregular form of the grains certainly supports this supposition as does also the appearance of the cell contents of the endosperm in which the various stages of the granulation are to be seen.

Ginkgo biloba.

After what has been said about the Cycads, there is no need to enter so fully into the details of *Ginkgo*, in which most particulars of the structure of the female gametophyte are extremely similar.

---

[1]) Zacharias, E., „Ueber d. chem. Beschaffenheit d. Zellkerns". (Bot. Zeit. 1881. p. 169 to 176.) „Ueber d. chem. Beschaffenheit v. Cytoplasma u. Zellkern". (Bericht. d. D. Bot. Ges. Bd. XI. 1893. p. 293—307.) „Ueber Nachweis u. Vorkommen v. Nucleïn". (Bericht. d. D. Bot. Ges. Bd. XVI. 1898. p. 185—198.)

The migration of the food also follows much the same course as in the Cycads. We had however a more complete series of materials of different stages of development after the formation of the starch grains in the endosperm, than we had for the Cycads, and will now summarise the results of observations on material collected at intervals of every 2—3 days. With *Ginkgo* there is great uniformity in the development of the different ovules on the same tree or even on different trees growing in the same place, so that more value attaches to dated observations for *Ginkgo* than for the Cycads where there is much irregularity even in one and the same cone.[1])

For this purpose we used principally microtome series, passed into water or alcohol as the case demanded, and examined in Iodine. In the course of one month (Aug. 28th to Sept. 30th) the changes were as follows. Beginning with a stage in which the endosperm cells in general contain-ed many starch grains, we found the grains smaller in the cells nearer the archegonia and a little larger in the cells of the jacket layer, while the egg cell was free from starch. In the next stage the grains in the jacket cells were smaller and stained a brownish rather than the true blue violet of the storage starch of the rest of the endosperm; very small brownish violet grains also began to appear in the egg cell. This difference in the nature of the starch in the sheath cells was also observed in permanent preparations of microtome series which had been stained with Flemming's triple stain from which the Gentian violet was almost entirely washed out. In these the large storage starch grains of the usual endosperm cells were stained pale flesh colour, while the grains in the jacket cells were blue. These reactions certainly show that the starch grains in the two regions were in somewhat different conditions, probably indicating that the starch in the jacket cells was just being transformed into soluble carbohydrate by diastase secreted in the jacket cells. In later stages the starch steadily decreased in the jacket cells, in which the grains were sometimes grouped together to one side of the cells in a curious manner (like the arrangement in the "statolith" starch grains) for which we have as yet no explanation. In these stages the number of starch grains in the egg increased. The jacket cells then emptied themselves of starch, beginning at the base of the Archegonium till they were finally completely emptied in about 3 weeks from the first mentioned date. The emptying of the cells of starch spread in an outward direction in the endosperm till the zone immediately round the archegonia for 10—15 cell layers was free from it, just as was the case in the Cycads (cf. figs 7 and 8). We judged in both cases from the various facts observed, that this starch, temporarily stored in the endosperm, was being transformed into soluble carbohydrate and passed into the egg cell.

---

[1]) Dr. Miyake informed us of great irregularity in the development of the ovules of *Zamia floridana*.

The protein grains have a very similar distribution, and in the general endosperm cells which were packed with starch grains, there were also almost as many large protein grains (see fig. 8, s.). At the time however when the starch grains were disappearing from the egg cell, the large protein granules remained in it. In *Ginkgo* as with the Cycads, it is most unlikely that protein grains travel as such from any of the surrounding cells into the egg, but are probably converted to some soluble simpler forms easier for transit by the action of Proteases[1]) and are re-deposited in the right place in a higher form for the immediate use of the growing egg or for temporary storage.

Pinus.

Between *Pinus* and the two groups just treated, the chief differences lie in the size of the ovule, which is relatively small in *Pinus*, and in the (perhaps consequent) very different relations between the state of development of egg and embryo, and the date of deposition of nutritive substances. To describe in detail chiefly from work on *P. Cembra, montana* and *sylvestris*, we find the case is as follows.

In very young ovules in which the archegonia were not present, starch was already deposited in considerable quantities in the tip of the nucellus, but was intirely absent from the endosperm tissues, in which however there was much sugar (glucose). After the first appearance of the archegonia, and all through their earlier stages this was also the case. The jacket cells of the archegonium are early differentiated and have extremely large nuclei, but no starch has been observed in them in any of these younger stages.

In the next important stage (the nucleus being in the middle of the egg) the cytoplasm of the egg cell had become very vacuolated with usual vacuoles, while it was still but little granular. From ovules in such a stage of development in *P. Cembra* material was collected every 3 hours and examined in a fresh condition, and at the same time some was fixed immediately. At 6 A.M. there were considerable numbers of small starch grains lying scattered in the cytoplasm of the egg (cf. fig. 9). Some grains were still present at 9 A.M., but in far fewer numbers, and by noon the cytoplasm of the egg was devoid of starch. In the afternoon the starch was observed at 3, 6 and 9 in small quantities. Quite similar results were obtained with *P. sylvestris* in ovules in a similar stage. At 1.30 midday there was no starch in the egg cells, while at 6 P.M. there were many fairly big grains scattered all through its cytoplasm.

This stage of development was passed over in a few days, and in *P. sylvestris* after 5 days the egg cytoplasm had become very granular and large numbers of true "protein vacuoles" were present.

---

[1]) Vines, S. H., „Tryptophane in Proteolysis". (Ann. of Botany. Vol. XVI. 1902. p. 1 to 22.) „Proteolytic Enzymes in Plants". (Ann. of Botany. Vol. XVII. 1903. parts I and II.) „The Proteases of Plants". (Ann. of Botany. Vol. XVIII. 1904. p. 289 to 316.)

Even in the fresh unstained condition most of the detailed structure of these "protein vacuoles" and the grains in the cytoplasm are to be clearly seen, particularly with the oil immersion, and they show a number of granules in each which react towards reagents as protein substance; thus we see that they are by no means the result of fixing as was suggested by Blackman[1]). Digestion experiments however, which yielded such satisfactory results with *Macrozamia* etc., were technically very difficult with *Pinus*, for on using sections of fresh material the vacuoles ran together so that the cytoplasm became uniformly granular even when left in pure water only for a short time. With prolonged treatment with the warm digestive fluid it was soon impossible to distinguish the granules of the protein vacuoles owing to the indistinct homogeneous appearance of the whole mass of cytoplasm, so that we were unable to determine the effects of digestion on the protein granules themselves. With fixed material on the other hand the granules appeared to have been rendered more resistant, and the chief granules in a protein vacuole were not digested even after a long time in the fluid. With acetic methyl green however, we found that the nuclei of the endosperm, jacket cells, and egg cell stained quite strongly, but that the protein granules in the egg cytoplasm and in the "protein vacuoles" were hardly stained, if at all. This shows that these protein granules differ from nuclei and have no nuclein as their constituent part.[2])

In some cases, and this appeared to be quite erratic, there were grains present in the protein vacuoles which were exceptionally refractive and which proved on staining to be starch grains (see fig. 10). Thus in the "protein vacuoles" we get not only protein substance, but also carbohydrate in the form of starch grains. For the present we propose the term "nutritive vacuoles" to replace "protein vacuoles", but we will have more to say later on this subject. It is interesting to note that in Hofmeister's[3]) original paper he figures the „Keimbläschen" so accurately as to appear as if he had observed not only the protein bodies but also the starch grains without recognising them. The starch grains we have observed in these vacuoles are always small, sometimes there being only one or two, sometimes several together. Though they are not by any means always present we have not been able to observe as yet any regular periodicity in their appearance corresponding to that in the earlier stages described.

In that stage of the ovule in which the contents of the pollentube are about to be discharged into the egg cell we found the following conditions. The nucellus tip was quite crammed with

---

[1]) Blackman, V. H., „Cytol. feat. of fertil. in *Pinus sylvestris*". (Phil. Trans. Roy. Soc. Lond. Ser. B. 1898. see p. 417.)

[2]) Zacharias, E., „Ueb. Nachweis u. Vorkommen v. Nuclein". (Bericht. d. D. Bot. Ges. Bd. XVI. p. 194—197.)

[3]) Hofmeister, W., „Vergleich. Unters. d. Keimung etc. höherer Kryptogamen ... u. d. Samenbildung d. Coniferen". Leipzig 1851. cf. plate XXIX. fig. 1, 3 and 4.

starch in a median zone, and the pollen tubes which reached almost to the egg were packed with large storage grains. In the endosperm cells at the base of the egg cell a few grains may have collected, but in the egg cell itself there were none. When the pollen tube had just discharged into the egg cell we found the large storage starch grains from it lying together in the tip of the egg or near the nucleus in the upper part, and in some cases half in and half out of the pollen tube. A little later these big grains lay scattered all through the cytoplasm of the egg, having been carried round by a streaming of the cytoplasm? These large grains were quite different in appearance from the transitory starch usually found in the egg cell, and they were speedily used up by it.

Thus there are at least three different series of starch grains to be found in the egg cell. a) The small grains scattered in the cytoplasm itself before the "nutritive vacuoles" are formed and which seem to be subject to daily periodicity. b) The small grains in the "nutritive vacuoles" the presence of which varies even among ovules of the same cone. c) The large grains brought by the pollen tube and speedily used up by the egg cell. All these grains of starch in the egg cell seem to be used up in the course of its activities.

After the formation of the embryo a number of the "nutritive vacuoles" still retained their normal appearance; even when the suspensors were so big as to carry the embryo to the very middle of the endosperm, they were to be observed intact, sometimes also with the starch grains in them. At this time there were but few starch grains in the suspensors themselves, and their cell walls (like that of the egg) contained amyloid, for in a fresh condition they stained bluish with iodine.

With the formation of the embryo, starch began to collect in the cells of the endosperm at the base of the egg cell and in the cells surrounding the embryo, but the endosperm as a whole did not get filled till very late.

The origin of the protein grains in *Pinus* as in the Cycads and *Ginkgo* is to be looked for in some forms of soluble protein compounds such as amides or hexonbases, which pass in through the endosperm from cell to cell. Whether or not the nucleoli of the jacket cells play an important part in working up the protein before its entry to the egg cell as suggested by Ferguson is difficult to say just yet. It does not appear to us to be quite reasonable to look for the sole supply of protein nourishment for the egg to the nuclei of the jacket cells; nor is Ferguson's[1]) view that secondary nucleoli develop in the egg to be the "nutritive spheres" to be easily accepted. Arnoldi's extraordinary results can be explained as suggested by Strasburger[2]) as due to

---

[1]) Ferguson, M. C., „Contrib. to the know. of the life hist. of *Pinus*". (Proc. Washington Acad. of Sci. Vol. VI. 1904 see p. 107.)
[2]) Strasburger, E., „Ueber Plasmaverbindungen pflanzlicher Zellen" (Jahrb. f. wiss. Bot. Vol. 36. 1901. p. 493—606. see p. 550—552.)

artifact or as abnormal phenomena. In the course of our work we have never observed any such phenomena in material fixed in alcohol nor in that fixed in Flemming's solution.

Structure of the wall of the central cell (later egg cell and ventral canal cell) in Cycads, Ginkgo and Pinus.

As the structure of the egg cell membrane in these three groups is the same in all essentials, it will be more convenient to consider them together.

By the time of Miquel[1]) and Warming[2]) the real nature of the egg-wall was not realised, although they noted that it was thick and pitted. The writers of the next period[3]), [4]) figured a membrane closing the deep pits on the side of the jacket cells, and the results of our present close examination have led us to confirm this view and not that of the more recent workers, eg. Ikeno[5]), Coulter and Chamberlain[6]), Smith[7]) and others who represent in their works merely broad open communications through the very thick egg membrane. Goroschankin's description is remarkably detailed and accurate. He noted that closing the deep pits of the thick wall of the egg is a fine membrane which is itself somewhat irregularly thickened and perforated in a way comparable to a sieve plate. He missed the final pit closing membrane however, and took the filling plasma of the smaller pits to be actual open communications of cytoplasm between the egg cell and jacket cells, so that his "sieves" are comparable to some of Kienitz-Gerloff's[8]) thicker plasmodesmen in other plants which were pointed out by Meyer[9]) not to be open communications but merely the pit filling plasma on either side of a fine lamella.

---

[1]) Miquel, F. A. W., „Nouv. mat. p. servir à l. conn. d. Cycadées". (Archiv. Néerland. III. 1868. p. 193—254. see p. 209 and pl. XI. fig. 6.)

[2]) Warming, M. E., „Recherch. et remarques s. l. Cycadées". (Overs. o. d. Kon. Dan. Vid. Selsk. 1877. french résumé p. 16—27.) „Contrib. à l'hist. nat. d. Cycadées". (Overs. o. d. K. D. Vid. Selsk. 1879. resumé 9—12. pl. VI. fig. 6 and 7.)

[3]) Goroschankin, J., „Zur Kennt. d. Corpusc. b. d. Gymnospermen". (Bot. Zeit. 1883. p. 825—831.)

[4]) Treub, M., „Recherch. s. l. Cycadées". (Ann. d. Jard. d. Buitenz. Vol. IV. 1884. pl. II. fig. 7—8.)

[5]) Ikeno, S., „Unters. ü. d. Entwick. ... b. *Cycas revoluta*". (Jahrb. f. wiss. Bot. XXXII. 1898. p. 557—597. see Pl. VIII.)

[6]) Coulter, J. M., and Chamberlain, C. J., „Morph. of Spermatophytes. Pl. I. Gymnosperms". New York 1901. p. 22.

[7]) Smith, I. S., „Nutrition of the egg in *Zamia*". (Bot. Gaz. Vol. 37. 1904. p. 346—352.)

[8]) Kienitz-Gerloff, F., „Die Protoplasmaverbindungen zw. benachbarten Gewebselementen in d. Pflanze". (Bot. Zeit. Jahrg. 49. 1891. parts 1—6 begin. p. 1.)

[9]) Meyer, A., „Das Irrthümliche d. Angaben ü. d. Vork. dicker Plasmaverbindungen zw. d. Parenchymzellen einiger Filicinen u. Angiospermen". (Bericht. d. D. Bot. Ges. XIV. 1896. p. 154—158.)

By staining alone it is extremely difficult to recognise the final closing lamella. As well as several other stains, Congored shows up the "sieve structure" very well, but chlorzinciodine owing to its deep staining property is the best. With this type of stain however it appears as though the pores of the sieve themselves represent the final open communications, which is due to the fact that the final closing membrane does not stain with cellulose stains. That there is such a difficulty in the staining of the pit closing membrane was already noticed by Russow[1]) and Gardiner[2]). According to Mangin[3]) the final pit closing membrane, which is the middle lamella, consists of pectin substance and is to be stained by a different series of staining substances than those used for cellulose. Among them ruthenium red[4]) is the most characteristic. We found however that even with the latter the final membrane is not very clearly demonstratable here owing to its extreme thinness, and consequently the small amount of stain it can take up. The thick part of the egg membrane stained very darkly, and then the "secondary" and "tertiary" thickenings on the wall of the "sieve" portion get gradually less and less dark till one can scarcely see the membrane across the final sieve pores (cf. fig. 3).

By swelling the lamella however, we were able to demonstrate its existence, as well as the fact that it is perforated by extremely fine pores, to see the actual plasmic connections, and also to determine the fact that the only actual plasmic communications between the cells are "plasmodesmen". The best material for the demonstration of these finest of threads we found to be *Encephalartos Lehmanni*, of which we used hand sections of alcohol material. These sections were washed in water, treated for a short time with H_2SO_4 and then deeply stained with aniline blue. In spite of the fact that it is very simple, this method gave very satisfactory results. The membranes were much swollen, and when examined with an oil immersion of strong magnification the sieve pores were seen to be closed by a very delicate lamella pierced by plasmodesmen in groups of 3 or 4 together (see fig. 1 and 2). Not only the middle lamella which constitutes the closing membrane of the finest sieve pores, but also the thicker portions of the closing membrane for the pits of 1st order, 2nd order and so on, we found to be traversed by the plasmodesmen. Thus plasmodesmen may be said

---

[1]) Russow, E. A. F., „Ueb. Tüpfelbildung u. Inhalt d. Bastparenchym- u. Baststrahlzellen d. Dicot. u. Gymnosp." (Sitzungsber. d. Naturforscher-Gesellschaft. Dorpat 1882. p. 350—389.)

[2]) Gardiner, W., „On the continuity of the protoplasm through the walls of veg. cells". (Phil. Trans. Roy. Soc. Lond. 1883. p. 827.)

[3]) Mangin, L., „Sur la constitution d. l. membrane d. végétaux". (Compt. Rend. Vol. 107. 1888. p. 144 to 146.) „Sur la présence d. composés pectiques d. l. végétaux". (Compt. Rend. Vol. 109. 1889. p. 579—582.) „Sur la substance intercellulaire". (Compt. Rend. Vol. 110. fig. 90. p. 295.) Sur les réactifs colorants d. substances fondamentales d. l. membrane. (C. R. Vol. 111. 1890. p. 120.)

[4]) Mangin, L., „Sur l'emploi d. rouge d. ruthénium en anatomie végétale". (Compt. Rend. Vol. 116. 1893. p. 653.)

to be distributed all over the irregularly thickened membrane closing the pits of the first order (cf. fig. 1 and 2 and diagram 4).

A similar arrangement of the plasmodesmen was seen in alcohol material of *Cycas*, *Zamia floridana* and others, although for the latter species Smith[1]) recently elaborated a new view regarding the mechanism of nutrition, claiming large open communications between the egg and jacket cells.

The thick wall of the egg appears to be composed of at least pectin substance, cellulose, and amyloid, for we find that with ruthenium red and other stains for pectin substance it stains deeply, as it also does with congored, chlorzinc iodine and other cellulose stains, while it goes bluish with simple iodine, indicating amyloid.

For *Pinus* practically all that we have stated about the egg cell wall in *Ginkgo* and the Cycads holds good.

Although Ferguson[2]) states that no pit groups as described by Goroschankin have been observed by her, yet Blackman[3]) noted a "very distinctly pitted wall" in *P. sylvestris*, and in our materials we found no difficulty in detecting the larger sieves; even in hand sections of young stages mounted in water and unstained they were quite easy to observe in tangential direction with so low a power as Zeiss B × 4. The surface view of the "sieves" and pit groups is quite similar to those in *Cycas* or *Gingko*, but the actual thickness of the wall is much less. Pits of the 2nd and 3rd degree have been observed quite clearly, and although we have not yet seen the plasmodesmen we are convinced that they exist. The chemical nature of the thick wall is apparently the same as in the Cycads and *Ginkgo*, containing at least pectin, cellulose, and amyloid.

The question arises as to the reason for the great thickness of this wall. We find on the whole that the larger egg cells have the thicker walls; for example in the cycads, where the egg cell reaches a length of 3 or more millimeters, the wall is sometimes 0.15 mm thick, while in *Ginkgo* with egg cells considerably smaller it is less than half that thickness, and in the relatively small eggs of *Pinus* we find the wall very much thinner though it is still thick in comparison with those of the endosperm cells. In *P. Cembra* which has an exceptionally large female prothallium the wall is thicker than in the others. The thick wall is probably accounted for all through the Gymnosperms by the need of support and protection for the extremely large and delicate egg, which might easily be crushed by the rapidly growing endosperm. Such a thickness would consequently make it difficult even for soluble food stuffs to pass into the egg, so that pits would be necessary. These pits however need by no means be large open communications.

---

[1]) Smith, I. S., „Nutrition of the egg in *Zamia*". (Bot. Gaz. Vol. 37. 1904. p. 346 to 352.)
[2]) Ferguson, M. C., loc. cit. see p. 94.
[3]) Blackman, V. H., „Cytol. feat. of fertiliz. and rel. phenom. in *Pinus sylvestris*". (Phil. Trans. Roy. Soc. Lond. Ser. B. 1898. see p. 399—400.)

Certain it is, that in all the Gymnosperms we have so far examined a thick pitted wall such as we have described is to be found, and it is remarkably uniform in its structure and appearance in all the genera.

General Conclusions.

In the endosperm cells packed with stored food stuffs we find large numbers of protein grains of considerable size in addition to the starch (cf. fig. 5 and 8) and, as we have already pointed out it would appear equally extraordinary to suggest that these grains either of starch or protein, forced themselves from cell to cell as such. The transit of carbohydrates as sugars has been known for long, and the work of Schulze, Vines and others has taught us that storage protein materials in seeds do not travel as such during germination, but are first split up by the action of enzymes to soluble simpler forms in which they pass from cell to cell and which are later rebuilt to protein substances with the addition of carbohydrates and mineral salts; and it is most probable that practically the same thing holds good while the food is accumulating in the young endosperm. Notwithstanding this we have found many groups of very small pits in the cell walls of the usual endosperm cells, the whole system of pits being just like that found in the wall of the egg cell itself except that the groups are smaller, and as the walls of the endosperm cells are thin, they are much less conspicuous than they are in the egg wall. In them too the pit closing membrane will be traversed by groups of plasmodesmen.

Now therefore, when in the egg cell itself (where its very thick wall renders the pits in it conspicuous) there are deposited starch grains and protein grains, why should one be any more ready to believe that the starch and protein stuffs entered the egg in this solid form than one is in the case of the endosperm cells?

The statement of some workers, that there are large open communications through the pits between egg cell and jacket cells is quite contrary to the facts we have observed, and the view that protein granules pass from cell to cell as such, is against the current acknowledged theories for the passage of food stuffs between two neighbouring cells. Similarly the passage of whole nuclei or large portions of them through the membrane closing the big pits, which is perforated only by plasmodesmen pores far too fine to admit even the individual chromosomes, (cf. fig. 1 and 2) must be looked upon as an abnormal phenomenon.

In this preliminary discussion of nutrition, we have confined our attention to certain carbohydrates and protein substance in general; but there are of course other important organic compounds such as amide, hexonbase, arginin etc. as well as inorganic salts to be considered in the physiology of nutrition of the egg. They will be treated in the second part of this research.

As a result of our comparative study of the Gymnosperms

already enumerated, we find that the following brief account holds good for all the cases we observed.

The egg cell, which acts as a point of attraction for the food stuffs, is supplied with soluble food passing in through the endosperm. While it is young and growth is rapid apparently the supply does not very much exceed the demand and no food is deposited in solid form. Later however the balance is reached and so soon as the supply becomes greater than the demands of the growing egg deposition in solid or semisolid form begins round it. In the case of starch, deposition *always* takes place first in the cells of the endosperm at the base of the archegonia. In different groups the relative time of deposition and the state of development of the egg may vary greatly, for example in the Cycads and *Ginkgo* both starch and protein substance are largely deposited in the endosperm before the growth of the unfertilized egg is completed, but in *Pinus* deposition is extremely slight in the endosperm even after the embryo has reached a considerable size.

In all cases, at some time or times in the course of its development we found both starch and protein substance deposited in the egg cell itself. The protein substance is early deposited in large grains in the egg of Cycads and *Ginkgo*, and some grains are still present even after the formation of the proembryo. Starch on the other hand is much more vacillating in the egg, and has the appearance of "transitory starch", being present in very fine grains which are largely of the nature of amylodextrine. Both starch and protein substance are deposited first in the perifery of the egg cell, but later they are found scattered throughout the cytoplasm, probably being carried round by an internal streaming. The formation of transitory starch grains along the perifery of the protoplast of the egg is at times very conspicuous, and is certainly the result of the conversion of diosmosable sugars into non-diosmosable starch immediately after the entry of the former into the egg cell. Similarly the entering proteid is deposited in grains near the perifery. By this means the concentration of the soluble food in the egg cell is kept constantly below that of the surrounding cells, which ensures a continual transfer into the egg, and at the same time prevents a too great concentration of osmotic substances in the egg cell itself.

If then the process of the entry of food is such as we have indicated, what is the chief *function of the jacket layer* which is so very well characterised, particularly in the lower Gymnosperms? As we have already mentioned in the Cycads and *Ginkgo* the supply of food in the early stages is greatly in excess of the demands of the growing egg, so that much is deposited in solid form, till, in fact, the endosperm cells are packed with it. Once the food in the surrounding cells is laid down in solid form, the egg cell is practically cut off from it unless there is some means of rendering it soluble, or transmitting it into easily diosmosable substances; and it is here that we think the jacket cells play an important part. Though the presence of a large quantity of stored food in the endosperm tissues does not necessarily mean that no soluble food passes through these cells to the egg cell, yet when cells become packed with stored food their chief function ceases to be that of passage cells, and the stored food itself is certainly not available in that form. So far as we can judge by the results obtained by treating living material with Gujac resin, the jacket cells secrete oxydase and diastase which dissolves the starch in the neighbouring cells as it is required by the egg. Further, we have observed how the endosperm cells surrounding the egg gradually lose their starchy contents as the egg cell grows (cf. fig. 8). A similar solution and disappearance of the protein grains in the endosperm also takes place and we think it is probable that proteases are also secreted by the jacket cells, but as yet unfortunately we have been unable to demonstrate their actual presence in these cells.

The regularity of the arrangement of the jacket cells, their large nuclei and thick cytoplasm rich in granular contents, all unite in supporting the view that they are glandular or secretory in nature, and act as go-betweens for the egg cell and the stores of food in the endosperm cells. To some of the very fine well marked granular bodies present in large numbers in the jacket cells we may look for the proenzymes or zymogenes.

It is interesting to compare this view of the jacket cells with the results of some observations on Angiosperms in which the antipodal cells are found to have an important part to play in the passage of food to the egg cell. Westermaier's[1] original view that the antipodals in the *Ranunculaceae* had an important nutritive function, was followed and confirmed by Osterwalder[2], Goldflus[3], Ikeda[4] and Lötscher[5] in other groups of Angiosperms. By all these workers the antipodals are supposed to have the power of obtaining for the egg cell and of passing on to it the food materials which are present in the surrounding tissue. It is to be remembered that phylogenetically the antipodals are generally supposed to represent the reduced prothallium tissue; so that antipodals and jacket cells are in a way homologous. The present existence and differentiation of the Antipodals in some Angiosperms is due to their similar physiological function performed by them, and which corresponds with that of the more definitely organised jacket layer in Gymnosperms.

When we come to the Pines we find the jacket cells less strongly differentiated than in the Cycads and *Ginkgo*, which we

---

[1] Westermaier, M., „Zur Embryologie d. Phanerog. ... u. d. sogen. Antipoden". (Nova Acta Acad. Leop. Carol. 57. 1. 1890.)
[2] Osterwalder, A., „Beitr. z. Embryol. v. *Aconitum Napellus*". (Flora. 85. 1898. p. 254—292.)
[3] Goldflus, M., „Sur la struct. et les fonct. de l'assise épithel. et d. antipod. chez l. Composées". (Journ. d. Bot. 12. 1898 and 13. 1899.)
[4] Ikeda, T., „Studies in the physiolog. funct. of antipodals in *Trycirtis hirta*". (Bull. Coll. of Agricult. Tokyo Imp. Univ. Vol. V. 1902.)
[5] Lötscher, P. K., „Ueb. d. Bau u. d. Funkt. d. Antipoden in d. Angiosp". (Flora. Band 94. 1905. p. 213—262.)

take to be the natural result of their lesser physiological importance in this group. Because, as we stated above the amount of deposited food stuffs in the endosperm previous to the formation of the embryo is small in *Pinus*, so that what the egg requires is already to hand in soluble forms in the surrounding cells, and the jacket cells have not got to be so active in preparing stored food for it; also the embryo is so early carried down through the jacket cells into the endosperm by the suspensors that the jacket cells can do but little for it in comparison with what the jacket cells can do for the proembryo of *Ginkgo* for example. In many of the higher Gymnosperms, the differentiation of the jacket cells is not very great and they may be but short lived, while in some cases they are hardly recognisable as specially differentiated from the surrounding endosperm cells. For example in *Thuja* as described by Land[1]) the jacket cells, which do not seem to be so much differentiated as in *Pinus* appear at the time of cutting off of the neck cells, and break down shortly after fertilization. Now in *Thuja* we found that so little solid food is deposited in the endosperm that even after the embryo has reached a considerable size the quantity of starch in the surrounding cells is very trifling.

In Land's[2]) account of *Ephedra* he describes in the gametophyte a basal "storage" region, and an upper archegonial region in which all the cells are very feebly organised and the jacket cell walls "never at any time thick, become so tenuous that they can scarcely be seen and evidently offer little resistance to the passage of food into the central cell"; these cells break down altogether at the time of fertilization. According to our view their lack of differentiation is correlated with the fact that the storage region is distant from the egg cell and they have therefore no immediate service.

We have not as yet had the opportunity of examining all the genera of Gymnosperms from this point of view so that it is quite possible that exceptions may exist and a well differentiated jacket layer be present even when there is no deposition of food near the egg; but in such a case there may be some other physiological significance for these cells.

Up to the present all the workers have laid much stress on the nuclei and nucleoli of the jacket cells alone as the direct source of nutrition of the egg cell. The facts now brought forward shew this view to be untenable. Every cell of the endosperm does its share of temporaryily storing and passing on the food to the egg, though apparently the jacket layer is specially active and it is possible that the nuclei of the jacket cells may play some important part in the working up of the soluble simpler compounds into

---

[1]) Land, W. J. G., „A morph. study of *Thuja*". (Bot. Gaz. Vol. XXXIV. 1902. p. 249—258.)

[2]) Land, W. J. G., „Spermatog. and oogen. in *Ephedra trifurca*". (Bot. Gaz. Vol. XXXVIII. 1904. p. 1—16.)

slightly higher forms before they pass into the egg, still however in a soluble form.

What then are the „Hofmeister Körperchen"? There are frequently vacuoles round the simple protein grains of the Cycads and *Ginkgo*[1]) and further we have observed starch and protein grains in close proximity in the egg cells of *Ginkgo*, *Zamia* etc. In *Pinus* the „Hofmeister Körperchen" are more conspicuous, and contain protein grains and often also starch grains in the later stages of development. It appears to us to be highly possible that the vacuoles surrounding these grains of food stuffs may have a digestive capacity, and may therefore have much the same function and origin as those developped round food particles in unicellular organisms such as *Amoeba* etc. In the general cytoplasm of the egg there are also numbers of granules many of which are protein grains identical in chemical reactions, form, and size, with those in the nutritive vacuoles, and it may be that they are stored there temporarily and are awaiting their turn for digestion.

Possibly the reason that these "nutritive", or "digestive" vacuoles have appeared to so many workers to be nuclei, or to have the appearance of nuclei, may be that in general they have judged them chiefly from their staining properties with usual stains, and from their superficial appearance. In microtome sections stained with Triple stain, the large protein grains certainly stain like nucleoli, and the small grains give the appearance of the nuclear net work. But if one uses fresh material, or hand sections of alcohol material, stained them with acid methyl green[2]) one sees a considerable difference in the staining properties of these grains and of true nuclei. Also the result of artificial digestion of the protein grains with pepsin glycerine indicates that they are a different form of protein substance from that composing the nucleolus. We may suggest that many of the tiny granules one finds always in large quantities in these vacuoles (cf. fig. 10) may have the nature of zymogens or proenzymes for both proteases and diastases and may be the source of the digestive properties of the vacuoles.

That the nutritive vacuoles are less developed and conspicuous in the Cycads and *Ginkgo* than in the higher Gymnosperms may be correlated with the fact that in the former the jacket cells are more highly developed than in the latter, and also with a certain difference in the form and properties of the food stuffs brought into the egg cell.

Although these views are the outcome of the observation of a large number of facts, there is perforce much in them that is suggestion to and that may be useful only in the present state of our knowledge and require modification as we continue our researches.

---

[1]) It is interesting to note that Goroschankin calls the protein grains in *Ginkgo* „Hofmeister Körperchen" in the description of plates in his russian paper. (Wiss. Schriften d. Moskauer Univ. 1880. Pl. VIII. fig. 87a.)

[2]) Zacharias, E., „Ueber Nachweis u. Vorkommen v. Nuclein". (Bericht. d. D. Bot. Ges. Bd. XVI. p. 194 and 197.) We used the stain both with and without the addition of sodium sulphate.

Summary.

We may sum up the chief results of the above observations and considerations as follows:

1. Even the delicate walls of the endosperm cells are pitted in much the same way as the wall between the egg cell and jacket layer of the endosperm.

2. In addition to starch large numbers of protein granules are present in the endosperm cells of *Ginkgo* and Cycads of quite the same character and appearance to those in the egg cell.

3. A *final pit closing membrane* is present in *each pit* between the egg cell and jacket cells, and this membrane as well as the thickened portion of the pits of 2nd and 3rd orders are *perforated only by plasmodesmen*. Thus any big open communication between egg cell and jacket cells is positively denied.

4. In no case have any wandering nuclei of the jacket or endosperm cells been observed; and even after the development of the embryo has already begun, the jacket cell nuclei retain there integrity.

5. As it would be absurd to suggest that starch travels as grains from cell to cell, so it is pointed out to be equally absurd to say that the protein grains do this, either between two cells of the endosperm, between endosperm cell and jacket cell, or between jacket cell and egg cell.

6. It is suggested that the jacket cells are glandular or secretory and render the storage food of the endosperm soluble and available for the developing egg. At the same time their possible activity in the synthesis of food stuffs of higher compounds from the supply of simpler forms is not to be disregarded.

7. The fact that the jacket cells are less differentiated in some of the higher Gymnosperms than in the Cycads and *Ginkgo* may be corollated with the fact that in their ovules there is very little or no storage of solid food stuffs in the endosperm near the growing egg cell, the jacket cells have ∴ less work to do than in those (Cycads and *Ginkgo*) where there is a large deposit of stored food round the undeveloped egg.

8. The well developed jacket cells of the Gymnospermic prothallium are considered the phylogenetic homologues of the Angiospermic antipodals, and attention is drawn to the similar function performed by them and the active Antipodals of some Angiosperms described by Westermaier and others.

9. Transitory small grained starch has been detected in the egg cells of Cycads, *Ginkgo* and *Pinus* and found in association with the protein grains and even in the nutritive vacuoles.

10. So far as we could see, the granular contents of the nutritive vacuoles have no nuclein among their constituents as in most cases they do not stain with acetic methyl green.

11. The chemical nature of the nucleoli and protein grains is found to be different, as shewn by the results of digestion experiments, supporting our view of their different origin.

12. It is proved that the „Hofmeister Körperchen" are not nuclei, and we think it unlikely they are intimately connected with nuclei. We suggest that they may be digestive vacuoles comparable in origin and function with the digestive vacuoles of lower organisms, which are formed as required round the temporarily deposited food in the egg cytoplasm.

In the course of these investigations we have worked in the botanical laboratories of the Universities of Manchester, London and München, and the alpine Laboratory of Mount Schachen; and we cannot express too strongly our best thanks to Professors Weiss, Oliver, and Goebel for innumerable helpful kindnesses. We are also indebted to many people for material which has been invaluable; in particular we must thank Mr Moore of Dublin, Prof. Chamberlain of Chicago, Dr. Miyake of Kyoto and Drs. Yabe and Hattori of Tokyo.

Manchester and Tokyo.

Explanation of plate.

All figures drawn with the aid of a camera lucida. For highest magnification Beck's $1/_{14}$th in oil immersion and Zeiss compens. ocular 12 were used.

Fig. 1. *Encephalartos Lehmanni*. Portion of the thick pitted wall between egg cell and jacket cells, shewing final pit closing lamella perforated only by Plasmodesmen. From hand section swollen with sulphuric acid. × 2200.
      w thickened wall.
      l lamella closing pit perforated by groups of plasmodesmen, cf. arrows *a* diag. 4.
      j contents of jacket cells.
      e contents of egg cell.

Fig. 2. *Encephalartos Lehmanni*. Same as fig. 1. Shewing plasmodesmen through the thicker portions of the pit closing membrane.
      t thicker portion of membrane cf. arrows *b* diag. 4.

Fig. 3. *Zamia muricata*. Surface view of a small portion of the thick wall between egg and jacket cells shewing groups of pitted areas. From microtome section tangential to egg cell. Stained triple. × 900.
      g group of pits. cf. diag. 4. pit to 1st degree.
      w thickest portion of wall. cf. diag. 4. A.
      w' irregularly thickened portions. cf. diag. 4. B.
      r radial walls of jacket cells.

Fig. 4. General diagram of thick pitted wall between egg cell and jacket cells. Pits of 1st degree represent a whole group, or pitted area (cf. fig. 3. *g*). Within this the wall is irregularly thickened giving pits of 2nd or more degrees; this wall may be pierced by plasmodesmen, arrows *b* (cf. fig. 2. *t*). Arrows *a* represent plasmodesmen of final pit closing lamella. (cf. fig. 1. *l*).

Fig. 5. *Zamia floridana*. Small portion of egg cell and adjacent endosperm cells, shewing pitted wall and distribution of starch and protein granules. From microtome series, stained iodine. $\times$ 240.
    e egg cell cytoplasm.
    z zone at edge of egg cell where minute starch grains lie very thickly.
    t thick pitted wall.
    j jacket cells, empty of starch.
    en endosperm cells, with *s* starch grains, *p* protein grains.

Fig. 6. *Zamia floridana*. Small portion of cytoplasm of egg cell, shewing protein and starch grains. From microtome series, stained with iodine. $\times$ 2200.
    p protein granules of various sizes, sometimes very irregular in shape.
    s groups of minute starch grains, apparently in plastid.
    ss solitary starch grain in cytoplasm.
    v usual vacuole.

Fig. 7. *Ginkgo biloba*. Low power drawing to shew relations of Archegonia to stored food in surrounding endosperm. From microtome series, triple stained. $\times$ 54.
    e egg cell with protein grains (represented by black dots).
    j jacket cells.
    d region of nearly empty cells round egg from which starch and protein has been dissolved.
    s storage region of endosperm containing starch (pale rings) and protein (black dots).

Fig. 8. *Ginkgo biloba*. Small portion from fig. 7. $\times$ 240.
    e egg cell, finely granular with large protein granules *p*, cytoplasm slightly contracted away from jacket cells.
    t thick pitted wall.
    j jacket cells, with large nuclei and many very fine red staining granules in dense cytoplasm.
    d endosperm cells empty of all stored food.
    d' endosperm cells with small partly dissolved starch and protein grains.
    s storage region with *p* protein and *g* starch grains.

Fig. 9. *Pinus Cembra*. Small portion of cytoplasm of egg cell, before the formation of digestive vacuoles. Shewing usual vacuoles and starch grains in cytoplasm. From hand section of fresh material stained iodine. $\times$ 350.
    s starch grains. *v* vacuoles.

Fig. 10. *Pinus sylvestris*. Small portion of cytoplasm of egg cell shewing digestive vacuoles („Hofmeister Körperchen") with protein and starch grains. From hand section of fresh material stained iodine. $\times$ 350.
    d digestive vacuole.
    p protein grains. *s*. starch grains.

Beihefte zum Botanischen Centralblatt Bd. XX. Abt. I.

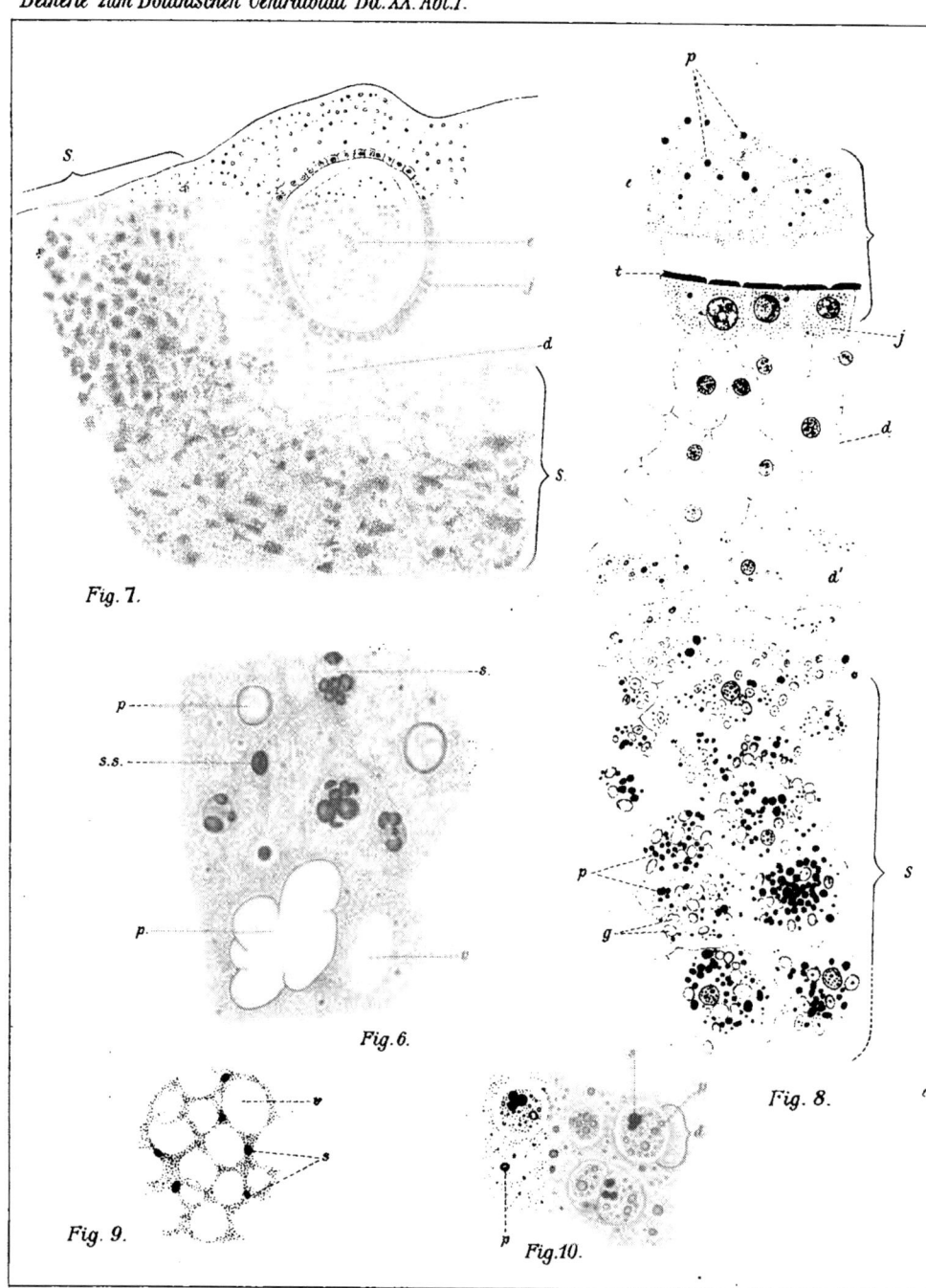

Stopes and Fujii del.
The Nutritive rel. of surround. Tiss. to Archeg. in Gymnosperms.

Verlag von C. Hein

Taf. I.

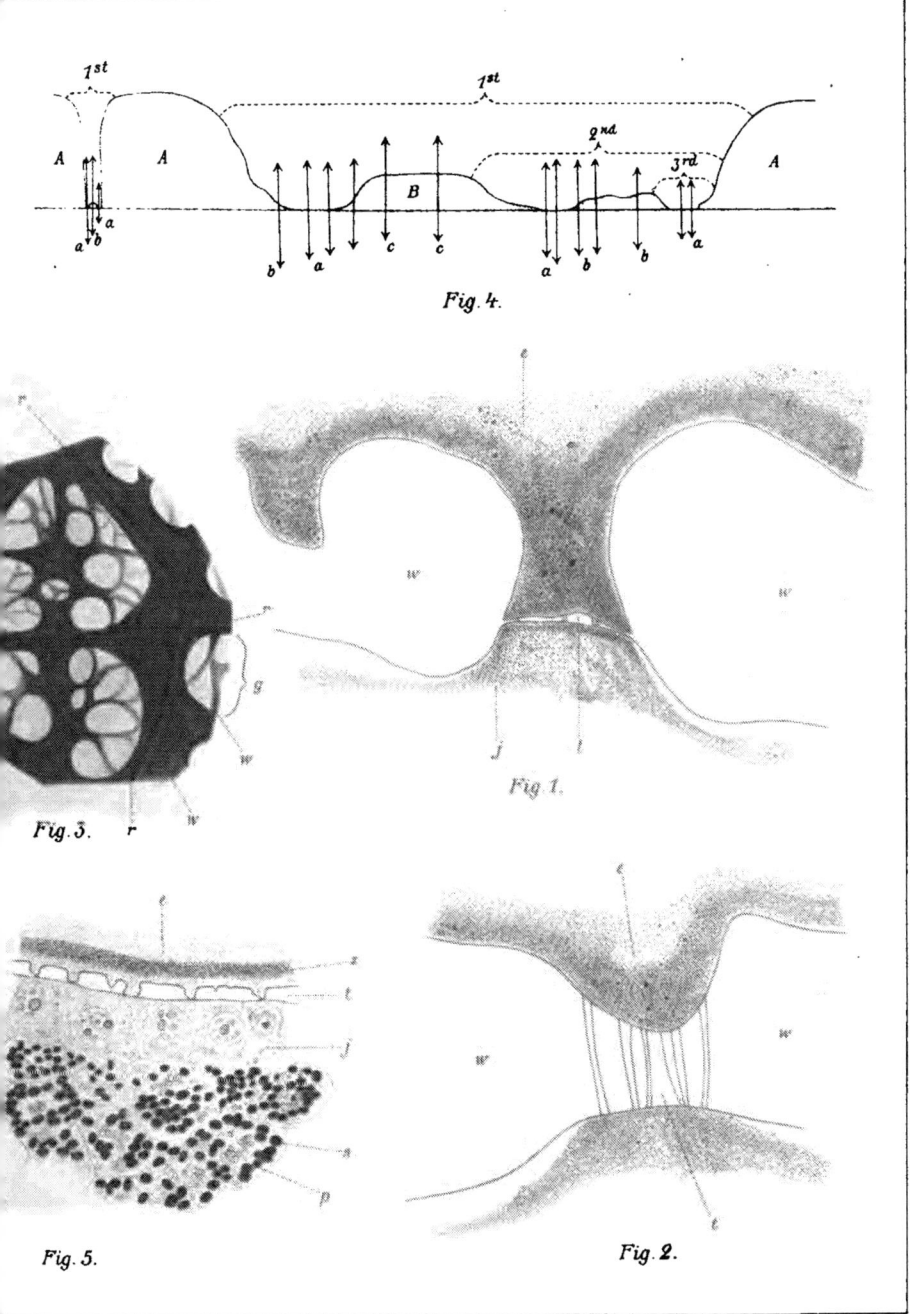

Printed by Libri Plureos GmbH in Hamburg, Germany